D0447662

Keep up with all the great adventures,
and don't miss a single experience!

Into the RAIN FOREST

by Jane Hammerslough

Based on the Animal Planet program
The Jeff Corwin Experience

SCHOLASTIC INC.

New York   Toronto   London   Auckland   Sydney
Mexico City   New Delhi   Hong Kong   Buenos Aires

If you purchased this book without a cover, you should be aware that this book is stolen property. It was reported as "unsold and destroyed" to the publisher, and neither the author nor the publisher has received any payment for this "stripped book."

No part of this publication may be reproduced in whole or in part, or stored in a retrieval system, or transmitted in any form or by any means, electronic, mechanical, photocopying, recording, or otherwise, without written permission of the publisher. For information regarding permission, write to Scholastic Inc., Attention: Permissions Department, 557 Broadway, New York, NY 10012.

ISBN 0-439-43565-X

Copyright © 2003 Discovery Communications, Inc. All rights reserved. Animal Planet logo, All Animals, All the Time and Animusings are trademarks of Discovery Communications, Inc.

All rights reserved. Published by Scholastic Inc.
SCHOLASTIC and associated logos are trademarks and/or registered trademarks of Scholastic Inc.

12 11 10 9 8 7 6 5   4 5 6 7 8/0

Printed in the U.S.A.
First printing, February 2003

Table of Contents

Introduction

With many different environments, including rain forests, wetlands, and volcanic islands, South America is home to animal species found nowhere else on the planet. If you've ever wanted to learn about animal extremes — the longest snake, the biggest rodent, or the largest parrot in the world — you've come to the right place.

We're about to embark on a journey that will take us to four exotic South American locations where these special animals — plus many, many more — can be found. With the help of *The Jeff Corwin Experience*, you can join Jeff and his friends as they travel through Panama, Ecuador, the Galápagos Islands, and Brazil. And all *you* need to do is keep reading this book!

From frogs that sound like cats to a species of wildcat that is an expert tree climber, from an otter that can grow up to 6 feet long to a rodent that is the size of a dog, from big birds with blue feet to tortoises that live for 150 years, the animals of these South American locations aren't just interesting — they are *incredible*.

Jeff's fascinating journey begins in the forests of Panama, home to unique monkeys, anteaters, lots of reptiles, and many other animals. We'll then travel south to mainland Ecuador, where we'll meet exotic kinkajous, tapirs, caimans, and several other unusual species.

From there we'll cross the water to the phenomenal Galápagos Islands, where giant tortoises roam, iguanas wander, and a remarkable group of penguins thrives. Finally, we'll explore the wildlife of the Pantanal region of Brazil, where rare giant otters frolic in rivers and a type of porcupine swings from trees.

So . . . what are you waiting for? If you're ready to meet some of the planet's most amazing animals, grab your sunscreen, hat, and shades — and join Jeff and the gang on their adventure to South America. First stop? Panama.

Experience Panama

Capital: Panama City.

Official language: Spanish.

Official name: República de Panamá (Republic of Panama).

Area: 29,157 square miles.

Elevation: The highest point is Volcan Baru, which is 11,401 feet above sea level.

Population: In 2002, the population was estimated at 2,938,000 people. Approximately half the population lives in cities and the rest in rural areas.

Chief products: Agriculture — bananas, rice, sugarcane, beef cattle, milk, coffee, corn, chickens and eggs, beans. Manufacturing — beverages, cement, petroleum products, processed foods. Fishing — shrimp, anchovetta.

Money: The basic unit is the balboa. One hundred centesimos equal one balboa.

Chapter One

Panama

Although it may be best known for the Panama Canal, one of the greatest human-made wonders of the world, the *natural* wonders of Panama should not be overlooked. The country's rain forests, mountains, and islands host a diverse group of animals that includes monkeys, anteaters, sloths, serpents, ocelots, and huge purple frogs!

The Panama Canal

Completed in 1914, the Panama Canal connects the Atlantic and Pacific Oceans. The canal extends 51 miles, from Limon Bay on the Atlantic Ocean to the Bay of Panama on the Pacific Ocean. It has three sets of locks — enclosed areas where the water level of the canal can be raised or lowered — so that ships can travel in both directions at once. Ships passing through the canal sail across Gatun Lake, a human-made lake created from an area that was once a valley covered by a rain forest. Now the tops of trees and hills rise up out of the water of Gatun Lake, creating islands that are primate sanctuaries.

Swinging Spider Monkeys!

For millions of years, monkeys have moved across the land in Panama, from north to south and south to north. In fact, Panama is the only place where you can find the Colombian species of spider monkey moving northward and the Central American spider monkey mov-

Science Note

• Colombian black spider monkeys grow between 16 and 21 inches in length — with tails that are from 28 to 34 inches long. On average, they weigh about 19 pounds.

• Spider monkeys have ridges on the underside of their tails for added grip.

• Because they make a lot of noise, spider monkeys are easy to find! When a stranger approaches, the creatures scream, bark, rattle branches, and even throw things!

• Spider monkeys are diurnal, meaning "active during the day." They forage for food in the morning.

• There are several different spider monkey species. As a group, their average life span is about 24 years — though in captivity some have reached 40 years old.

Science Note

The spider monkey got its name because it sometimes hangs upside down, with all four of its limbs and its tail holding a branch. In this position, the monkey resembles a huge spider.

ing southward! Jeff calls this movement of species "the great funnel exchange."

Spider monkeys live in trees and eat fruit, leaves, spiders, and other insects. With very long legs and an extremely flexible, prehensile — grasping — tail that can hold

JEFF'S JOURNAL
ON NIGHT MONKEYS AT NIGHT!

"They run around, hopping from branch to branch, from tree to tree. They're foraging sap. They're foraging for fruits and tender shoots. They're eating insects. They're even eating small animals."

tightly on to a branch and even pick up things, spider monkeys are some of the most nimble primates of all!

With four fingers that grip firmly, spider monkeys can easily swing through trees. But, as Jeff pointed out, they don't have a thumb. Why? When you're reaching out to grab a branch in midair a thumb would get in the way.

Night Monkeys

As Jeff discovered, some of the smallest monkeys in the world live in Panama. The night monkey, also called the black-headed owl monkey, weighs just 1 kilogram. The night monkey is from 9 to 15 inches long and has a tail 12 to 16 inches long. It is covered with grayish fur, except for its face. The center of its face is brown, with a white border and large white patches over the eyes. But perhaps the most striking thing about the night monkey is its huge eyes. These eyes are adapted to seeing in the dark and have earned the night monkey its other name — owl monkey.

The night monkey is the only nocturnal monkey in the world and can be found from Panama to northern Argentina. During the day, night monkeys rest in tree hollows, but when the sun sets they come out to forage for food. Night monkeys eat fruits, leaves, insects, and, occasionally, small mammals, reptiles, or birds.

Scientists have discovered that night monkeys seem to be most active during a full moon, but no one knows why.

Scorpions!

If you ever thought that scorpions live only in dry, remote deserts, think again. One of the largest species of the arachnid with the sting-

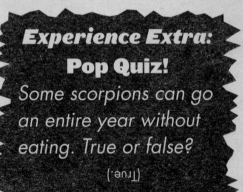

Experience Extra: Pop Quiz!

Some scorpions can go an entire year without eating. True or false?

(True.)

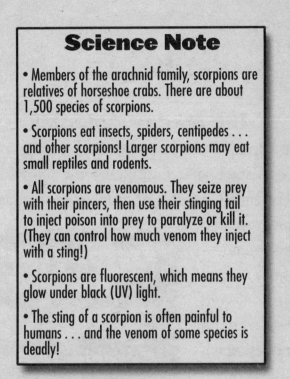

Science Note

• Members of the arachnid family, scorpions are relatives of horseshoe crabs. There are about 1,500 species of scorpions.

• Scorpions eat insects, spiders, centipedes . . . and other scorpions! Larger scorpions may eat small reptiles and rodents.

• All scorpions are venomous. They seize prey with their pincers, then use their stinging tail to inject poison into prey to paralyze or kill it. (They can control how much venom they inject with a sting!)

• Scorpions are fluorescent, which means they glow under black (UV) light.

• The sting of a scorpion is often painful to humans . . . and the venom of some species is deadly!

ing tail — the *Centruroides* — lives in Panamanian forests!

About 4 inches long, the *Centruroides* scorpion lives in crevices in tree trunks and beneath vegetation on the forest floor. But watch out . . . it's also sometimes spotted in buildings occupied by humans.

The Mighty Anteater

When a tropical rain forest borders a city, even large animals can sometimes find their way into human habitats. In Panama City, Jeff encountered an anteater that had wandered into someone's home — their kitchen, in fact. Jeff's mission? To bring the creature back to its own home — without harming it or letting it harm him. Luckily, Jeff was able to help

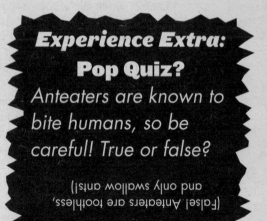

Experience Extra: Pop Quiz?

Anteaters are known to bite humans, so be careful! True or false?

(False! Anteaters are toothless, and only swallow ants!)

capture this particular anteater — called a *tamandua* in Spanish — and release it back into the wild. Unfortunately,

JEFF'S JOURNAL
ON ANTEATERS EATING!

"When it's time for these animals to feed, they'll approach a termite nest or anthill, and they'll start to dig and dig and dig. They stick their muzzle in there, [and] that tongue starts picking up stray ants. And they might only eat for a few minutes, because what they're doing is they're eating the more delicate ants. Because what happens then is the soldiers come out, the ants that are larger and specialize in defense and that can deliver bites and stings. So this creature will either close his eyes and tolerate it for a little bit, or move off and then possibly return back to the nest. An extraordinary creature, primitive in design, but perfect for survival in this tough ecosystem!"

Science Note

Anteaters may look slow and lazy, but they can move quickly, and when cornered they will fight. These animals don't have teeth, but they do have long, curved claws on the ends of each of their toes. In fact, they walk on their knuckles because their claws are so long. These claws can be used to fend off a potential predator, to climb trees, or to tear apart logs to uncover food. In addition, anteaters have prehensile tails and short legs.

many such encounters end with the animal badly hurt, or worse, dead.

Long-noses Rule?

Panama is home to another long-nosed animal, but this one may not look quite as unfamiliar as the anteater. That's because the coatimundi — also called the coati or the hog-nosed coon because of its long nose — is related to the raccoon.

Science Note

• Anteaters are part of a group of mammals called *Xenarthrans* found in Central and South America. They range in size from 20 inches to nearly 7 feet long.

• Although their eyesight and hearing are not well developed, anteaters can smell something as far away as a half mile!

Meet the Coati

Coati have long, pointed muzzles,

long, bushy, ringed tails, and brownish fur. They range in size from 13 to 27 inches long plus their tails, which can be just as long as their bodies. They weigh from 7 to 15 pounds. Males are larger than females. The females live in groups of four to 24 individuals called bands. Males join the bands only during the mating season. Coati have been known to live for 14 years in captivity.

In the wild, coatimundi live in tropical rain forests, grasslands, and brushy areas of South America and southern North America. They are excellent tree climbers. In fact, they can reverse their ankles — turn them around — so that they can climb down trees headfirst.

Coatimundi are diurnal and spend most of the day foraging for food. They are omnivores, meaning that they eat both meat and plants. They eat small prey like lizards, insects, rodents, snails, and birds, as well as fruit and nuts. They often eat while hanging upside down from a tree branch. A coati finds food using its keen sense of smell.

Super Sloths!

Sloths spend a lot of time hanging in trees — upside down. In fact, this creature eats, sleeps, and even gives birth upside down!

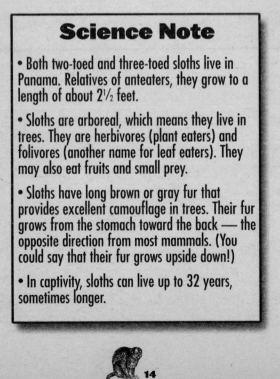

Science Note

• Both two-toed and three-toed sloths live in Panama. Relatives of anteaters, they grow to a length of about $2\frac{1}{2}$ feet.

• Sloths are arboreal, which means they live in trees. They are herbivores (plant eaters) and folivores (another name for leaf eaters). They may also eat fruits and small prey.

• Sloths have long brown or gray fur that provides excellent camouflage in trees. Their fur grows from the stomach toward the back — the opposite direction from most mammals. (You could say that their fur grows upside down!)

• In captivity, sloths can live up to 32 years, sometimes longer.

Furry Algae?!

During the rainy season, sloths sometimes take on a greenish-blue hue. This is due to algae that grow in their fur. This algae is found nowhere but on two-toed sloths.

"Not only do they harbor this unique species of algae in their fur, but they also harbor a moth that lives in this fur and nowhere else, and eats the algae," Jeff explains. "So you have an animal living in a complex ecosystem, this tropical rain forest, and in itself, it's a complex micro-ecosystem, home to all sorts of flora and fauna!"

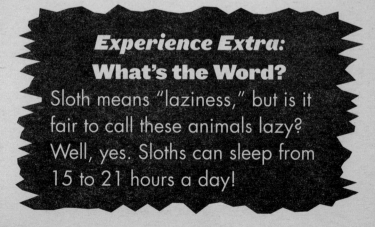

Experience Extra:
What's the Word?

Sloth means "laziness," but is it fair to call these animals lazy? Well, yes. Sloths can sleep from 15 to 21 hours a day!

Incredible Tree-climbing Cats

Millions of years ago a land bridge now called the Isthmus of Panama rose out of the ocean. Some animals, like armadillos, used the bridge to head north, ending up in North America, while other animals went south. One of those animals is the ocelot. This beautiful feline

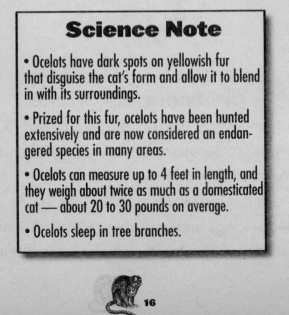

Science Note

• Ocelots have dark spots on yellowish fur that disguise the cat's form and allow it to blend in with its surroundings.

• Prized for this fur, ocelots have been hunted extensively and are now considered an endangered species in many areas.

• Ocelots can measure up to 4 feet in length, and they weigh about twice as much as a domesticated cat — about 20 to 30 pounds on average.

• Ocelots sleep in tree branches.

is the largest of the small-bodied wildcats — a group that also includes margays, jaguarundis, and tiger cats. All are much smaller than large cats like tigers, lions, or jaguars, but these are *not* house cats.

As comfortable moving along tree branches as they are on the ground, ocelots are fearsome hunters. They will go anywhere for prey, from swimming in rivers for turtles, fish, and frogs to chasing birds and tree rats high above ground!

The Spearlike Snake

The Bothrops Asper snake is also called the fer-de-lance — which refers to the shape of the animal's head. It looks like a spear, or lance.

A member of the viper family, the fer-de-lance has long, hollow fangs and potent venom. Like its relative the rattlesnake, it vibrates its tail when it is disturbed, but

Science Note

- The Bothrops Asper, or fer-de-lance, can grow as long as 8 feet, though most are only 4 or 5 feet in length.

- The animal's body is brown or dark gray, with a black-edged diamond pattern.

- At night, the animal comes out and lies on warm roads.

- Fer-de-lance snakes can give birth to litters of about 80 baby snakes at one time! Even new-born snakes have dangerous fangs and venom.

it doesn't have a rattle.

Rotating Fangs

The fer-de-lance's fangs aren't just long and filled with venom — they can also *rotate*! These types of fangs are called *solenogly-phus*. Jeff explains, "They can rotate; they're opposable. They can be retracted or they can extend outward."

Makeup, Anyone?

In addition to the fer-de-lance, Panama is home to another very unusual serpent: the eyelash viper. These snakes can grow from 18 to 30 inches in length, and their bodies can be reddish-yellow, yellow, grayish-brown, or green. The yellow color may be spotted with white, black, or red; the darker colors can be spotted with black or red. But what makes the eyelash viper most interesting are the supraciliarie, or enlarged scales, above each eye that make the vipers look like they have eyelashes. While its coloration is excellent camouflage, its "eyelashes" are also camouflage, because they make it difficult for potential prey — and

Experience Extra:
Heat-sensing Serpent

Like rattlesnakes and copperheads, the fer-de-lance has thermal receptor sites — or holes — just below its nostrils. This allows the snake to detect the warmth that radiates from warm-blooded prey, like rodents and birds.

predators — to see the snake's head among the sur-rounding foliage.

This viper is arboreal — it lives in trees — and has a prehensile tail. When catching and eating food, it can hold on to a branch with its tail and hang com-pletely suspended in midair while eating its entire meal. Vipers eat small mammals, lizards, frogs, and birds. They are nocturnal and like to live in wet forests with lots of shrubs, brush, vine tangles, trees, and palms for camouflage. They can be found throughout southern Mexico, Colombia, Ecuador, and western Venezuela.

A Purple or Poisonous Frog?

When Jeff traveled to an area of Panama called the Dar-ién, he encountered a couple of incredible frogs — one was huge and purple, and the other was *poisonous*.

**Experience Extra:
About the Darién!**
Although people tried to settle parts of the jungle area known as the Darién about a hundred years ago, the jungle resisted — and eventually won! Today, the only human residents there are some biologists.

Smokey Jungle Frog!

This amphibian can grow to be 7 inches long or bigger — and that's *big* for a frog. It lets out a loud squeal when threatened. And the smokey jungle frog, or *Leptodactylus pentadactylus* specimen that Jeff encountered in a cave, is purple.

The frog Jeff met is also big and muscular. As he says, "He's got pectoral muscles . . . and [huge] arms.

Out in the forest, you'd find these guys eating insects. But in this cave system, they're eating *bats!*"

Poison Dart Frogs

On the other end of the size spectrum is the tiny poison arrow, or poison dart, frog. One of the smallest species of its kind, the animal has an excellent defense mechanism: a deadly toxin in its skin! When eaten, the frog's poison enters a predator's bloodstream, and the predator dies.

Between the swift cats, slow-moving sloths, and poisonous frogs, Panama has been an amazing experience. Now it's time to head south to Ecuador, home to some more incredible creatures, including the largest snake on Earth!

Science Note

The Choco Indians used poison from these frogs for hunting animals such as deer, monkeys, jaguars, iguanas, and birds. They would collect poison from the frogs and then dip their arrow tips into it. Once the arrows were dry, they were ready to use for hunting.

JEFF'S JOURNAL
ON POISON DART FROG PARENTS

"The male transports his tadpoles on his back. Its back is bubbling, bubbling with life, bubbling with a new generation of poison dart frogs. And with some species, they will take those little tadpoles after they hatch, and then they'll transport them to good locations for them to grow up!"

Experience **Ecuador**

Capital: Quito.

Official language: Spanish.

Official name: República del Ecuador (Republic of Ecuador).

Area: 109,484 square miles.

Elevation: The highest point is Chimborazo Volcano in the Andes Mountains, which is 20,561 feet above sea level.

Population: In 2002, the population was estimated at 13,090,000 people. Approximately two-thirds of the population live in cities and the rest in rural areas.

Chief products: Agriculture — bananas, beef, cacao, corn, milk, coffee, oranges, potatoes, rice, sugarcane, wheat. Fishing — shrimp, herring, mackerel. Forestry — balsa wood. Manufacturing — cement, processed foods, straw hats, textiles. Mining — petroleum.

Money: The basic unit is the United States dollar. One hundred cents equal one dollar.

Chapter Two
Ecuador

Ecuador is named after the equator, the imaginary line dividing Earth's hemispheres that runs through the northern part of the country. Ecuador is home to some fascinating animal extremes, from the largest and longest snake on the planet and one of the

Experience Extra:
About Ecuador

Although it is just 110 square miles, Ecuador has a remarkable range of environments, from sunny beaches to jungles to snowy mountains. It's possible to travel from the tropics to the ski slopes in just an hour or two.

biggest crocodilians anywhere to tiny, intriguing ants and millipedes.

Meet the Tapirs

The first creature Jeff encountered in Ecuador was a tapir — a long-nosed creature related to rhinos and horses that weighs upward of 140 pounds. Tapirs are perfectly designed for survival. In fact, they haven't changed in 20 million years.

Excellent swimmers and divers, tapirs can lay low

Science Note

• Tapirs are born with a pattern of stripes and dots over their bodies. One scientist described them as "watermelons with legs"!

• Tapirs are found in Central and South America.

• An endangered species, tapirs have long been hunted for their tough hide but are now legally protected.

Kinkajou

Spider monkey

Eyelash viper

Night monkey

Anteater

Fer-de-lance

Sloth

Poison dart frog

Toucan

Caiman

Ocelot

Giant river otter

Emerald tree boa

Leafcutter ants

Hyacinth macaw

Tortoise

Penguins

Marine iguana

Seal pup

underwater, using their muzzles as snorkels. By sinking down below the water's surface, they can hide from predators such as jaguars and pumas.

Ants and Millipedes

Some of Ecuador's most fascinating animals are also some of the smallest. Ecuador is home to many different

Experience Extra:
Pop Quiz!

Ants are social animals that live in large colonies, work together in an organized way, and communicate with one another through scent. True or false?

(True.)

JEFF'S JOURNAL
ON A LEAFCUTTER ANT — OR ATTA — CITY

"*Fungus is what these ants live off: it is their food . . . [But] some of the leaves have been cast aside. Why is this leaf being wasted? All that work went into harvesting this leaf. Reason why? It probably contains a fungicide. A fungicide inside an atta city is death to the entire colony!*"

insects — including at least 95 different species of butterfly — and new species are being discovered.

Amazing Leafcutter Ants

The leafcutter ants that Jeff encountered are part of a large, complex community of creatures. Thousands of ants travel miles into a forest and follow a trail of chemicals up a tree to a canopy of leaves. Then they cut, collect, and transport the leaves back to their home.

Why? To make edible fungus! Back in the nest, ants mix leaves with a fluid from their bodies that creates a special ant food — a fungus found nowhere else in the world.

"Armored" Millipedes

The word *millipede* means "1,000 legs." Although no millipede really has that many limbs, some species of these bugs have 750. The insect's pairs of legs move together as it walks.

Found in rain forest ground litter, millipedes are herbivores that are harmless to humans. To protect themselves from predators, they have special defense mechanisms such as

Experience Extra: Millipede Scent

The millipedes that Jeff found in Ecuador give off a scent like bitter almonds.

tough plates on their bodies that act like armor. These insects also give off an unpleasant scent that protects them.

Snakes, Snakes, Snakes

From enormous anacondas to incredible Amazon tree boas to graceful green vine snakes, Jeff found a host of incredible serpents in Ecuador.

The Biggest Serpent on Earth

Quick — what's over 30 feet long, has no fangs, swims quickly, and eats everything from small birds to whole

---

Science Note

• Anacondas are nocturnal, hunting at night by waiting for prey to come near — then striking.

• Anacondas squeeze the air from their prey, but rarely crush their victims' bones.

• Anacondas are between 2 and 3 feet long at birth.

---

deer? If you answered "anaconda" or "water boa," you're right.

This snake uses constriction to kill prey. Then, with special jaw ligaments that allow the snake to open its mouth very wide, it swallows prey whole and headfirst. Powerful acids in the snake's stomach help it to digest its meal.

Amazon Tree Boas

If you ever see a four-foot constrictor dangling down from a branch in the Amazon jungle, it just might be an Amazon tree boa.

This particular species of snake has unusual eyes. As Jeff explains, "It has elliptical pupils. During the nighttime, those pupils widen out. During the daytime, they're

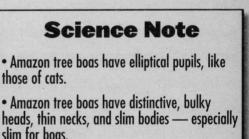

Science Note

• Amazon tree boas have elliptical pupils, like those of cats.

• Amazon tree boas have distinctive, bulky heads, thin necks, and slim bodies — especially slim for boas.

• Amazon tree boas move between the ground and trees, eating rodents, lizards, and insects.

just little slits, cutting out as much of the light as possible." Its pupils work something like natural, built-in sunglasses for the serpent.

Who's the Biggest?

The anaconda, python, and boa constrictor are all members of the same reptile family, *Boidae* or constrictors. They all get big, but which one is the biggest?

The anaconda can grow as long as 29 feet, but the reticulated python rivals it for the title of longest snake. Reticulated pythons have reached 33 feet in length! However, the anaconda wins when weight is taken into consideration. In fact, a 20-foot anaconda can weigh more than a 33-foot python. Anacondas can weigh 550 pounds or more, but will usually top out at a few hundred pounds and measure more than 12 inches in diameter.

At a mere 6½ feet to 11½ feet in length and 30 to 40 pounds in weight, the common boa constrictor doesn't even come close to its two bigger relatives.

Science Note

- Vine snakes are slow moving, with mild venom.
- When threatened, the vine snake puffs up the front of its body and opens its mouth wide to make itself look bigger.
- Most vine snakes are about as thick as your index finger.
- These serpents are diurnal, which means they are active during daylight.

Vine Snakes

About 6 feet long, the slender green vine snake stretches out between branches of trees — incredibly well camouflaged!

Able to lift half of its body into the air and so flexible it

Experience Extra: Pop Quiz!

Animals that look and act like vine snakes — but have completely different origins — are found all over the world. True or False?

(True.)

can coil into a tight ball, this beautiful serpent hunts birds, lizards, and other tree-dwelling prey.

Kinkajou: "Honey Bear" of the Rain Forest

The small, furry, golden-brown kinkajou is also known as a "honey bear." Found in trees in rain forests through-

JEFF'S JOURNAL
ON MOSQUITOES AND FUR

"I've always wondered why animals in the tropics have such thick fur. I think, is it a gene of extinction? And now I've discovered thick fur is an excellent way to keep mosquitoes at bay."

out Central and South America, this relative of the raccoon weighs about 5 pounds and has a prehensile tail and a catlike face.

A nocturnal animal, the kinkajou spends days sleeping in tree hollows. The

Science Note

• Kinkajous eat fruit and nectar as well as tree frogs, birds, and insects. Their predators include ocelots, jaguars, and foxes.

• A kinkajou drinks nectar with its 5-inch-long tongue. They help distribute pollen by moving from flower to flower as they feed.

• Kinkajous use a musklike scent to mark territory.

• The kinkajou's voice ranges from a soft coo to a loud scream.

kinkajou often perches upside down, grasping tree branches with its strong tail and hind claws. In fact, this animal can rotate its hind feet out and turn them backward so that the bottom of the feet and the claws can more easily grasp a branch.

Science Note

- Black caimans can swim with only their eyes above the surface of the water, but they can also see underwater because they have special protective membranes in their eyes.

- Black caimans have 75 long, sharp teeth to catch prey, but they swallow prey whole.

- Female black caimans build 5-foot-tall mounds of dirt and vegetation as nests in which to lay their eggs. They lay about 50 eggs at a time.

Seeking the Black Caiman

The black caiman is one of the world's largest reptiles, growing up to 20 feet long. Jeff de-

Experience Extra: Pop Quiz!

Black caimans are diurnal, which means they are most active during the day. True or false?

(False. They are nocturnal, active at night.)

scribes this crocodilian as secretive, shy, beautiful — and an important part of why the lagoons of Ecuador are so special!

Close relatives of alligators, caimans have rounded snouts, webbed feet, and long, muscular tails that help to propel them through the water. Skilled swimmers, they live in rivers, lakes, and other freshwater habitats. They eat fish, turtles, frogs, birds, mammals . . . and even other caimans.

Now that we've experienced some of the fascinating mammals, insects, and reptiles of the mainland of Ecuador, it's time to head offshore to the Galápagos Islands. This string of incredible islands, part of Ecuador since 1832, is home to a host of iguanas, birds, and other amazing animals found nowhere else on the planet!

Experience the Galápagos Islands

Capital: Quito (the Galápagos Islands are part of Ecuador).

Area: 3,029 square miles.

Islands: The Galápagos archipelago (string of islands) is made up of 13 large islands, six smaller ones, and dozens of islets and rocks. The largest islands are Isabela, Santa Cruz, San Cristóbal, Fernandina, San Salvador, and Santa María.

Population: In 2002, the population was estimated at almost 20,000 people. Every year, more than 60,000 tourists visit the islands as well.

Galápagos National Park: Created by Ecuador in 1959 to help protect the environment, the park includes more than 90 percent of the islands' land area. In 1986, the surrounding waters were set aside as the Galápagos Marine Reserve, and in 1998 that reserve was extended to protect the waters 40 miles from shore.

From extraordinary iguanas to enormous tortoises, the Galápagos Islands are famous for animals that have evolved in completely unique ways. Part of Ecuador and located 600 miles from the mainland, the Galápagos archipelago is comprised of more than 100 islands. Their isolation and constant volcanic activity have provided a unique habitat for thousands of years.

Amazing Evolution, Incredible Iguanas

Ancestors of Galápagos reptiles are thought to have originally drifted to the islands on "rafts" of vegetation from mainland rain forests. Over many thousands of years, those animals changed, evolving into distinct species suited to survive in the rocky, saltwater environ-

Experience Extra:
About the Galápagos Islands!

In 1835, naturalist Charles Darwin sailed to the Galápagos and used the islands to illustrate his theories on the origin of species. Darwin was one of the first scientists to explore the idea that animals evolve, or change and adapt as a means of survival, over time.

ment. Even more amazing, groups of iguanas developed in different ways on different islands!

Marine Iguanas

On the Galápagos Islands, typical green rain forest iguanas have evolved into saltwater survivors that range in color from coppery green and red to black, depending on the island. Species range from less than a foot to 3 feet long. Marine iguanas eat saltwater algae, and they swim, though they are most comfortable on land.

Over time, marine iguanas developed some very special characteristics to help them adapt to life on land and in water. For example, marine iguanas have longer, sharper claws than land iguanas, and flatter tails (to help with swimming). And because they spend time in a saltwater environment, they've had to learn how to deal with that, too. Marine iguanas have developed glands that collect salt from their bloodstreams. They then sneeze to expel salt water from their nostrils. The spray often falls back on their heads, creating a salty white "wig." While these adaptations make marine iguanas unique, they are still lizards, and must therefore regulate their body temperatures by collecting and storing heat. So after a dip in the ocean, large groups of them can be found lying in the sun getting warm. Marine iguanas are a great example of an animal that's adapted to what could have been extremely harsh surroundings.

JEFF'S JOURNAL
ON IGUANAS' FEW PREDATORS

"We're in the Galápagos. . . . Something that many of the creatures living here in this archipelago share . . . is they have unique adaptations with regard to the way they're built or their behavior. But one behavior they do not possess is a fear of predation — because animals have been allowed to evolve for millions of years on these islands without the impact of a creature coming to eat them."

As Jeff says, "[Iguanas] are the only lizard in the world that can actually survive in . . . and harvest their food from the marine environment. Amazing reptiles found nowhere else but the Galápagos!"

Land Iguanas

Isabela is the largest island in the Galápagos archipelago, and it's home to some of the largest iguanas in the world. As Jeff describes them, "[It's] like I'm staring face-to-face with a T-rex, but this is no dinosaur. This is a very modern, beautiful lizard. A land iguana."

Three feet long and weighing more than 30 pounds, Galápagos land iguanas are strong, muscular animals that can live for 60 years — twice as long as their saltwater relatives.

Male land iguanas are extremely colorful. They are copper colored along the body, with a yellow head and underside and red eyes. Like marine igua-

Science Note

• Each island in the Galápagos hosts a different species of marine iguana: All are closely related, but vary in size and coloration depending on their environment.

• The life span of a marine iguana is about 30 years.

• To identify and defend their own territory, marine iguanas bob their heads and open their mouths wide before charging and fighting each other.

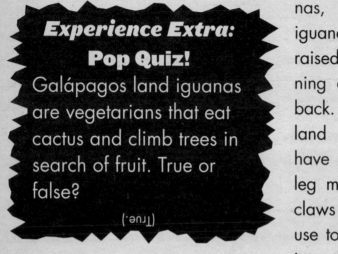

Experience Extra: Pop Quiz!

Galápagos land iguanas are vegetarians that eat cactus and climb trees in search of fruit. True or false?

(True.)

nas, male land iguanas have raised spines running down their back. Female land iguanas have powerful leg muscles and claws that they use to dig down into the ground to build nests. The female lays between two and 25 eggs in the burrow at one time, and fiercely defends her turf from other iguanas. Young land iguanas hatch in three to four months.

Has there ever been an iguana that was part-land and part-marine iguana? Yes, there is evidence of cross-breeding between the two species. In fact, Jeff encountered just such a *hybrid* — the offspring of genetically different parents — during his time on the island of Isabela. How did he know that what he was seeing was a hybrid? The first thing he noticed was that this particular iguana was very black, just like the marine iguanas. But it also showed some whitish pigment, just like what can be found on the neck of a land iguana. In addition, this particular iguana had a round, flat muzzle just like a marine iguana. Marine iguanas need that flat muzzle for grazing on seaweed or algae. What's next for this hybrid breed? No one knows for sure. As Jeff says, "We really don't know where this is going to go. . . . [This could be] an animal that will be totally unique . . . with its own characteristics for survival. . . . Or maybe it's something else. Maybe it's an experiment that ends here. . . . Who knows? To get the real answer, stick around for a couple of thousand years."

Great Galápagos Sea Lions

About 50,000 Galápagos sea lions live on the island of Plaza Sur. Weighing as much as 550 pounds, these are

Science Note

• Galápagos sea lions are excellent swimmers capable of diving hundreds of feet below the surface of the water to capture squid and other prey.

• Sea lions communicate with one another by loudly barking and roaring.

• Aside from sharks, Galápagos sea lions have few predators.

some of the largest animals on the islands. Galápagos sea lions live in colonies of about 30 animals. Each colony is led by a male known as a bull.

Young Galápagos sea lions, or pups, live together in a rookery. The pups spend their days napping, playing, feeding, and practicing their swimming skills in shallow pools near the beach. As Jeff explains, "When it's time for them to venture out on their own, when it's time for them to be independent, they have all the behavior they need to survive."

Equatorial Penguins?!

If you think that penguins can only survive in frosty places, think again. One of the planet's smallest penguin species lives on the island of Mariela in the Galápagos — 6,000 miles from Antarctica.

Staying Cool — and Warm!

Scientists believe that the penguins living in the Galápagos are the descendants of those that made their way north from Antarc-

---

Science Note

• Galápagos penguins use both their feet and their flippers to move around their rocky islands. On smoother ground, the birds hop.

• Predators of penguins in the Galápagos include sharks, seals, and sea lions. The other major threats to the animals are overheating or hypothermia.

• The penguins have excellent camouflage to avoid predators: Their black coats help them blend into their dark lava rock environment.

• Many scientists believe that Galápagos penguins developed from a cross between the Humboldt and the Magellan penguin species.

JEFF'S JOURNAL
PENGUIN PARENTS

"These penguins make excellent parents. These babies will be raised by their parents for nearly a year. And these penguins invest so much energy into the rearing of their offspring that the offspring can weigh up to a quarter kilogram [1 kilogram is about 2.2 pounds, so a quarter kilogram is just over half a pound] more than the parents — because the babies do nothing but sit here and eat. They sit, they wait, and they grow!"

tica millions of years ago. As they adapted to their new environment, the birds evolved into a distinct species.

Cold water currents surround the islands where Galápagos penguins live, providing the animals with lots of sardines, mullet, and crabs to eat. But because these penguins divide their time between the icy waters and the hot island shores, they have had to develop new behaviors to regulate their body temperatures.

To stay cool on land, the birds walk around with their wings held out at 45-degree angles to allow air to circulate around their bodies. To stay warm in the water, the birds constantly preen — smooth or clean — their dense feathers, so that they're compact and well lubricated. When the penguins are swimming, these features are the only barrier between their skin and the icy water!

The Birds Known as Boobies

The Galápagos are home to a fascinating group of birds known as boobies. Because they sometimes strike funny poses, the birds may have been named after *bobo*, the Spanish word for clown!

It's All in the Family — or Not!

If you think it's hard living with your brother or sister, well, at least you're not a boobie.

Science Note

• Three species of boobies are found in the Galápagos: the blue-footed boobie, the red-footed boobie, and the masked boobie, named for a featherless area around its bill.

• During mating, blue-footed boobies do a dance involving their distinctive blue feet. The male keeps raising one foot, then another, until he attracts a female.

• After mating, the male boobie builds a nest — which the pair doesn't use! Instead, the female scrapes away the nest and lays eggs on the bare ground.

• Boobies are amazing hunters, capturing fish by "dive-bombing." They fly into the sky — up to 80 feet high — stop suddenly, then hurl themselves headfirst into the water!

After the female boobie lays her eggs, the parents create a ring of guano (bird excrement) around the nest area. This ring separates one nesting area from another. If a boobie chick wanders outside this ring, or if its sibling "pushes" it out of the ring, its parents will ignore it — forever. Scientists aren't sure why boobies act this way. It may be that this behavior evolved to prevent parents from raising another pair's young. It also may be a way to ensure that the strongest boobie chick survives.

Huge Tortoises

Galápago is a Spanish word for saddle. The rounded shells of huge tortoises on the islands off the coast

Science Note

• The shell of a Galápagos tortoise is about 4 feet long. The largest fossilized shell ever discovered was 7 feet long.

• Tortoises have existed for more than 185 million years.

• These large reptiles are herbivores that have a beak but no teeth. Their diet consists of leaves, grass, fruit, flowers, grass, and cactus.

• The animals are believed to be adults — able to reproduce — beginning at the age of 40!

• Hunted by humans for their meat and oil for many centuries, Galápagos tortoises are an endangered species that is now protected.

JEFF'S JOURNAL

ON EVOLUTION AND THE GALÁPAGOS ISLANDS

"Galápagos is an extraordinary place. To be called 'a living laboratory of evolution' is appropriate indeed. It has brought scientists for years and years, first Darwin and then the others. And they come to better understand our world in this amazing process of evolution!"

of Ecuador reminded Spanish explorers of galápago saddles — so they named the tortoises, and the string of islands, Galápagos! Celebrated by Charles Darwin, the huge, dome-backed Galápagos tortoise is perhaps the most famous symbol of the islands.

Weighing as much as 700 pounds, the Galápagos tortoise is the largest tortoise in the world. With a life expectancy of *150 years*, this animal is one of the planet's longest-living vertebrates as well!

Extraordinary examples of adaptation and evolution, the animals of the Galápagos Islands are like no others in the world! For now, we'll say *adios* to the unique penguins, iguanas, tortoises, and the other fascinating animals of the Galápagos archipelago. We're heading west to the Pantanal region of the magnificent country of Brazil, where giant rodents swim alongside giant reptiles!

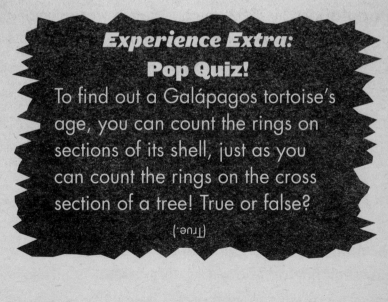

Experience Extra:
Pop Quiz!

To find out a Galápagos tortoise's age, you can count the rings on sections of its shell, just as you can count the rings on the cross section of a tree! True or false?

(True.)

Experience Brazil

Capital: Brasília.

Official language: Portuguese.

Official name: República Federativa do Brasil (Federative Republic of Brazil).

Area: 3,300,171 square miles. Brazil is the largest country in South America, extending over half the continent and bordering 10 other countries.

Elevation: The highest point is Pico da Neblina, which is 9,888 feet above sea level.

Population: In 2002, the population was estimated at 174,222,000 people. Approximately three-quarters of the population live in cities and the rest in rural areas.

Chief products: Agriculture — bananas, cacao, cattle, coffee, corn, oranges, rice, soybeans, sugarcane. Manufacturing — automobiles, cement, chemicals, paper, rubber, steel, textiles, machinery. Mining — bauxite, beryllium, chrome, diamonds, gold, iron ore, magnesite, manganese, mica, petroleum, quartz crystals, tin, titanium. Forest products — Brazil nuts, carnauba wax, latex, timber.

Money: The basic unit is the real. One hundred centavos equal one real.

Chapter Four

Brazil's Pantanal

The Pantanal region of Brazil is the world's largest wetland area. Annual flooding alternates with a dry season that results in lush grasslands — and an incredible array of habitats and wildlife. Millions of

Experience Extra:
About the Pantanal

The lowland area of Brazil, the Pantanal borders the Paraguay River, extending to the western edge of the Brazilian plateau. An area the size of New England — about 84,000 square miles — the Pantanal is home to more than 100 species of mammals and reptiles.

migratory birds visit the area each year, and it's home to the world's largest rodent, huge tarantulas, and a rare, oversized river otter. All in all, the Pantanal supports a diverse group of animals.

Capybara: World's Largest Rodent

Science Note

• Capybaras are excellent swimmers and divers.

• Fast runners, capybaras have front legs that are shorter than their rear legs.

• These large rodents are an important source of food for jaguars, pumas, caimans, and anacondas in South America.

• The capybara is also called a carpincho, or water hog.

Question: What's got reddish fur, webbed feet, a blunt snout, a small head and tail, a big body, and is part of the rodent family? No, it's not a guinea pig! But if you think of an animal that's a little like a guinea pig — but weighs more than 100 pounds — you can imagine the capybara.

At about 4 feet long and 2 feet tall at the shoulder, the capybara is the largest rodent on the planet. Found near rivers, ponds, lakes, and swamps in the Pantanal and throughout other areas of South America, the capybara is a herbivore that thrives on grasses and other water vegetation — and loves to eat melons!

JEFF'S JOURNAL
ON FRIENDLY CAPYBARAS

"Capybaras are extremely social. It's not very common that you find an individual hanging out in a solitary fashion.... They often live in herds. They're extremely gregarious!"

Big Birds!

The Pantanal is a stopping point for millions of migratory birds — as well as home to the biggest toucans and the largest, rarest macaws in the world.

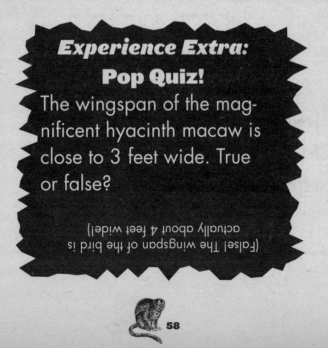

Experience Extra: Pop Quiz!

The wingspan of the magnificent hyacinth macaw is close to 3 feet wide. True or false?

(False! The wingspan of the bird is actually about 4 feet wide!)

Hyacinth Macaws

The hyacinth macaw has deep violet-blue plumage, and, at an amazing 40 inches tall, it is about the size of a four-year-old child, and the largest parrot in the world! Because there are only about 3,000 hyacinth macaws left in South America, it is also the rarest species of parrot anywhere.

Why are there so few of these birds? Hyacinth macaws eat only one thing: palm kernels. Loss of habitat where palms grow has contributed to the declining numbers of the species. Additionally, for years this beauti-

Science Note

• There are about 350 species of parrots in the world.

• Hyacinth macaws weigh about 2½ pounds.

• Hyancinth macaws mate for life and spend more than a year raising their young.

• In the Pantanal, hyacinth macaws nest in hollows in large trees.

ful bird was hunted for its flesh and feathers, and for the illegal exotic pet industry.

Unfortunately, loss of habitat, hunting — one bird

can sell for $10,000 or $12,000 — and its limited food source are pushing the hyancinth macaw toward extinction. Now that these birds are considered an endangered species, they are legally protected.

Toco Toucans

All over the world, toucans are instantly recognizable because of their enormous, colorful bills. The Amazon basin is home to the Toco toucan, which is the biggest toucan of all! Two feet tall, with big bright orange, yellow, red and/or blue beaks, and black bodies, these striking, loud birds nest in hollow trees in the Pantanal.

Like other birds, Toco toucans feed their young by

Science Note

• The colorful bills of Toco toucans are believed to attract mates. The bird uses the serrated — jagged — edge of its beak to cut up fruits and berries to eat.

• Because of their large beaks and bodies, Toco toucans are awkward flyers, and spend most of their time in trees.

• One of the bird's best defenses is its loud, screeching voice. Flocks of Toco toucans scare away other birds with extremely noisy, jeering calls.

• Toco toucans fold their tails and lay their bills on their backs when they go to sleep.

finding food, swallowing it . . . and then regurgitating it into their babies' mouths. Baby toucans eat a soup of fruit and insect or animal parts.

Tarantula Time!

Sure, you may have found some large spiders lurking under the sink in your bathroom, but did you know that some tarantula species have leg spans as wide as dinner

Experience Extra: Pop Quiz!

To defend themselves, tarantula spiders hurl barbed bristles from their abdomens at predators. True or false?

(True!)

plates? Imagine finding *that*! Brazil is home to many varieties of tarantulas, the largest type of venomous spider on the planet.

Science Note

• Tarantulas have an exoskeleton, or external skeleton, that is like a suit of armor. As it ages, the spider grows a new exoskeleton and molts, or sheds, its old skeleton.

• Tarantulas cannot chew food.

• Some tarantulas have abdomens the size of tennis balls!

• Tarantulas have sticky pads on their feet that can help them climb trees.

With two large front fangs and a big hairy body, a tarantula looks scary. But actually, it is a shy animal. Although its venom is potent, it is only deadly to its prey, which includes insects, young birds, frogs, mice, lizards, and other small animals.

The Porcupine with a Grasping Tail

Living in forests and low-lying jungle areas throughout South America, the prehensile-tail porcupine is like the porcupines of North America, but there are some important differences. For example, this animal has a long, grasping tail that it uses as a "fifth limb" to hang and swing from trees. In fact, this animal is *arboreal,* which means it spends most of its time in trees.

Although extremely agile when it comes to mov-

JEFF'S JOURNAL
ON TARANTULAS' "MILK SHAKES"

"He grabs on to prey, he sinks those fangs in, injecting the prey with venom that not only immobilizes and kills the prey, but also promotes digestion. The animal that this creature is eating actually dissolves into a spider frappé or milk shake, and then he just drinks it up!"

ing through trees, prehensile-tail porcupines are clumsy on the ground. However, with their 2½-inch-long spines, or quills, they are generally protected from such predators as ocelots. The only parts of the porcupine that are not covered in quills are its face, belly, and tail.

> ## Science Note
>
> • With a head and body that is about 12 inches long, prehensile-tail porcupines are smaller than their North American cousins.
>
> • To defend itself, the animal rolls into a ball!
>
> • The animals are herbivores, eating leaves, fruits, and seeds. Their nimble movements and relatively small size enable them to search for seeds at the very tips of tree branches.

Prehensile-tail porcupines are very nearsighted. However, the animals have excellent senses of hearing, touch, and smell. These porcupines have very large brains. Some scientists believe they have an excellent ability to remember things!

JEFF'S JOURNAL
ON A PREHENSILE-TAIL PORCUPINE

"Now, the defense works like this. He's not an aggressive animal. It's an herbivore. . . . It just sits and waits for stupid predators, like myself, to come in and think, Oh, here's a little animal that will make a nice meal. And they reach out and grab them and discover a pincushion of pain awaits!"

Giant River Otter

Ever see an otter? It's a cute, playful, furry animal that lives in rivers and is about the size of a raccoon. Now imagine this: an otter that is 6 *feet long* and weighs up to 80 pounds. That's the giant river otter, one of the rarest animals in the world — and found only in the rain forests and wetlands of South America.

The Mighty Water Dog

Also called a water dog, the giant river otter is the largest otter in the world. A close relative of the mink, the giant river otter is an intelligent, fiercely territorial animal. As Jeff explains, "Match an otter to a caiman and the otter will win every time. In fact, otters eat caimans!"

After encountering porcupines that swing like acrobats through the air, the world's largest spiders and rodents, rare birds, and even rarer mammals, it seems safe to say that the animals of the Pantanal in Brazil are an awesome group!

Our journey with Jeff and the gang has taken us through the rain forests, wetlands, and volcanic islands of South America, but now it's nearly finished. We've traveled down rivers, through swamps, and over oceans to find some truly remarkable animals. But wait, there's more!

How much do *you* remember about the rodents, reptiles, and other animals you've met on this incredible trek? There's just one way to find out, and it begins by turning the page!

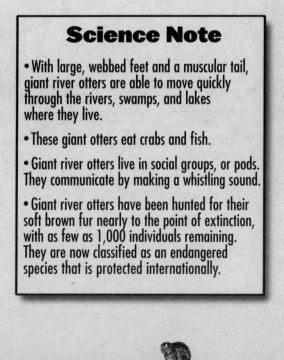

Science Note

• With large, webbed feet and a muscular tail, giant river otters are able to move quickly through the rivers, swamps, and lakes where they live.

• These giant otters eat crabs and fish.

• Giant river otters live in social groups, or pods. They communicate by making a whistling sound.

• Giant river otters have been hunted for their soft brown fur nearly to the point of extinction, with as few as 1,000 individuals remaining. They are now classified as an endangered species that is protected internationally.

Experience Quiz:
INTO THE RAIN FOREST

You've encountered some sloths in Panama, caimans in Ecuador, iguanas in the Galápagos, toucans in the Pantanal region of Brazil . . . plus a whole lot of other South American animals. So, what do you *remember* from your experiences? Here is where you can find out.

1. The birds found on the Galápagos Islands include
a. green-footed boobies.
b. loony boobies.
c. blue-footed boobies.

2. The kinkajou is also known as
a. fuzzy bear.
b. honey bear.
c. mini bear.

3. Anteaters walk on their
a. tiptoes.
b. knuckles.
c. claws.

4. From leg tip to leg tip, the world's largest tarantulas can grow as large as
a. a tennis ball.
b. a dinner plate.
c. a Volkswagen.

5. Galápagos turtles are named after a Spanish word for
a. clown.
b. island.
c. saddle.

6. The Bothrops asper is a relative of the
a. boa constrictor.
b. caiman.
c. rattlesnake.

7. The capybara is the world's largest
a. reptile.
b. mammal.
c. rodent.

8. On his back, the male poison dart frog transports
a. tadpoles.
b. lily pads.
c. its mate.

9. The life span of marine iguanas in the Galápagos Islands is about
a. 20 years.
b. 30 years.
c. 40 years.

10. The giant river otter can grow to be
a. 6 feet long.
b. 8 feet long.
c. 10 feet long.

Answers: 1.c, 2.b, 3.b, 4.b, 5.c, 6.c, 7.c, 8.a, 9.b, 10.a.

GLOSSARY

Agile [AJ-uhl]: able to move easily or quickly.

Arboreal [ahr-BOHR-ree-uhl]: dwelling in trees.

Archipelago [ahr-kuh-PEHL-uh-goh]: a string or group of islands.

Canal [kuh-NAL]: a human-made watercourse for transportation or irrigation.

Descendants [dih-SEHN-duhnts]: offspring of a certain ancestor.

Diurnal [deye-ER-nuhl]: active during the day.

Evolution [ehv-uh-LOO-shuhn]: the process of development, formation, or growth that occurs over many generations as planets and animals adapt to survive.

Folivore [FOH-luh-vohr]: leaf eater.

Herbivore [ER-buh-vohr]: plant eater.

Hybrid [HEYE-bruhd]: the offspring of genetically different parents, especially the offspring produced by breeding animals of different species.

Isthmus [IS-muhs]: a narrow strip of land that connects two larger land areas.

Nocturnal [nahk-TUHR-nuhl]: active at night.

Preen: to smooth or clean feathers with the beak or bill.

 72

GLOSSARY

Prehensile [pree-HEHN-suhl]: grasping, usually by wrapping around an object.

Primates [PREYE-mayts]: an order of mammals that includes man, apes, monkeys, and other animals.

Regurgitate [ree-GUR-juh-tayt]: to throw up partially digested food.

Venom [VEH-nuhm]: poison produced by some snakes, insects, and spiders.

Vertebrates [VUHR-tuh-bruhts]: a group of animals that have a backbone and/or spinal column.

All photographs copyright © Discovery Communications, Inc. unless otherwise noted.

CREDITS Color insert page 1: Kinkajou © Michael_Patricia Fodgen/Minden Pictures; Spider Monkey © Rod Williams-naturepl.com; Page 2: Anteater © Michael_Patricia Fodgen/Minden Pictures; Page 3: Fer-de-Lance © Peter Oxford-naturepl.com; Page 4: Toucan © Frans Lanting/Minden Pictures; Page 6: Giant River Otter © Frans Lanting/Minden Pictures; Page 7: Hyacinth Macaw © Frans Lanting/Minden Pictures